Finns and Amazons

Nancy Mattson

ARROWHEAD
PRESS

First published 2012 by
Arrowhead Press
70 Clifton Road, Darlington
Co. Durham, DL1 5DX
Tel: (01325) 260741

Typeset in 11pt Laurentian by
Arrowhead Press

Email: editor@arrowheadpress.co.uk
Website: http://www.arrowheadpress.co.uk

ISBN 978-1-904852-33-9

Printed and bound in Great Britain by
MPG Books Group, Bodmin and King's Lynn.

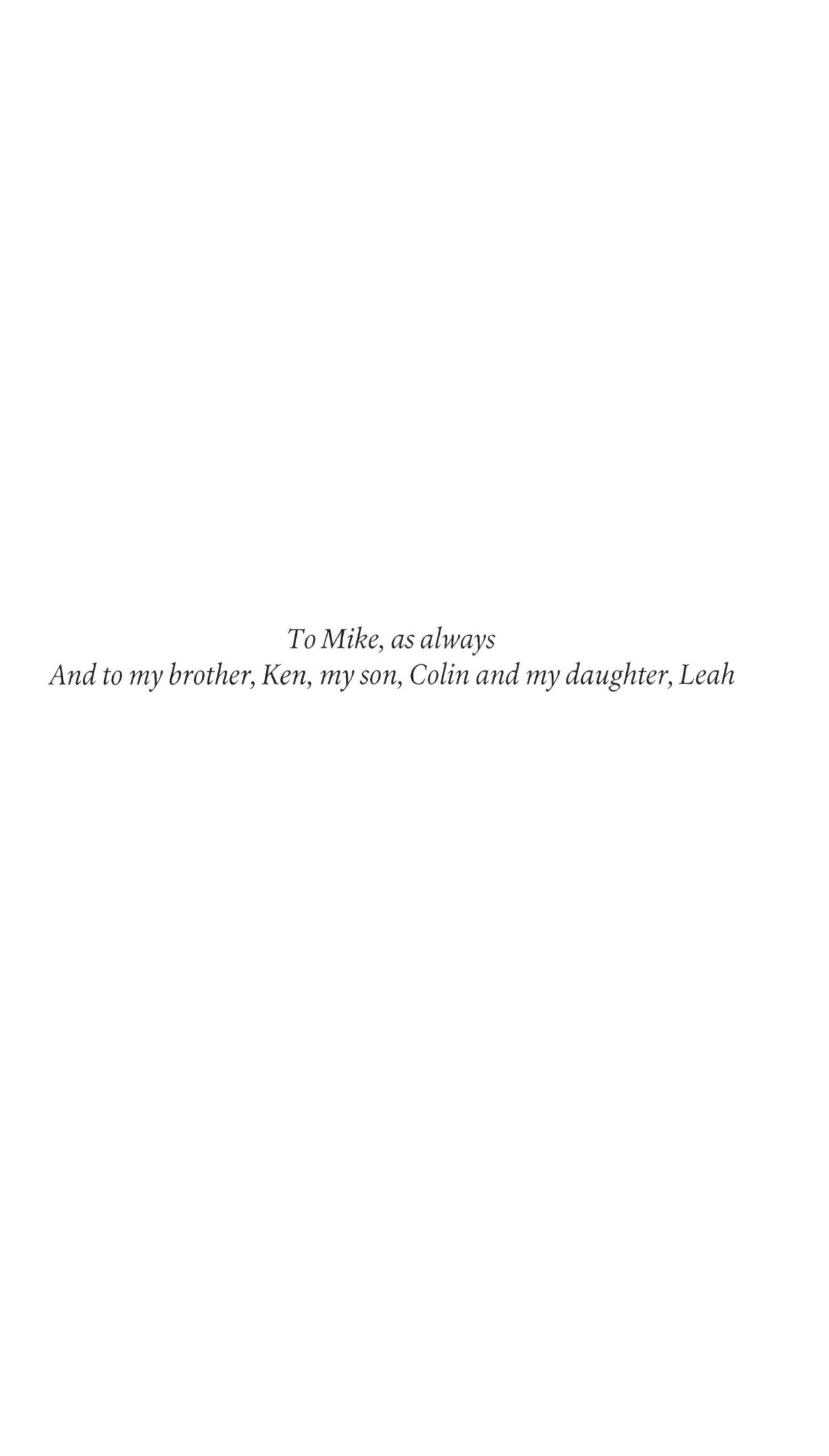

To Mike, as always
And to my brother, Ken, my son, Colin and my daughter, Leah

CONTENTS

III LETTERS

IV LEGACY

FOREWORD by the author

This book began with poems inspired by some early 20th century Russian women artists but developed mysteriously to include a poetic search for my Finnish great-aunt Lisi, who disappeared in 1939 in Stalinist Russia.

Six Russian women artists – Exter, Goncharova, Popova, Rozanova, Stepanova and Udaltsova – first gripped me at London's Royal Academy exhibition 'Amazons of the Avant-Garde' in 2000. But no poems emerged until 2003 in Paris, where I saw Sonia Delaunay's 1909 painting 'La Jeune Finlandaise'. I loved her fauvist portrait of a pre-adolescent girl but its title puzzled me until I discovered that Sonia was not French but born in Ukraine and raised in St Petersburg by a wealthy uncle with a dacha in Finland. Here was a personal link, a reason beyond art that Sonia and the 'Amazons' hooked me. They were neighbours of the Finns, whose blood is mine. They were of the same generation as my Finnish grandparents, born in the late 19th century. The first poems about Sonia and her milieu emerged.

Poems in the first part of *Finns and Amazons* respond to these Russian women pioneer artists who broke with convention as individuals and in creative collaborations with husbands, partners and friends in St Petersburg, Moscow and Paris. Moving beyond easel painting, they integrated art and life and became textile, fashion and industrial designers, book designers and illustrators, theorists and critics, teachers, photographers, stage and costume designers for theatre, films and ballet. Some experimented with poetry, others worked closely with poets. Most lent their skills to the revolutionary cause; none escaped political turmoil except through exile.

When my grandma Anna and her sister Lisi began to appear in the poems, the book shifted from artistic territory into fraught historical and family territory between Finns and Russians, especially in the borderland of Karelia. Anna and Lisi had emigrated with their parents from Finland to Canada before World War I. Anna settled in Saskatchewan, a pioneer farm wife with eight children, but Lisi joined thousands of North American Finns swept up in 'Karelian fever' who chose to move to Soviet Russia to help build a communist utopia. Anna and Lisi exchanged letters from 1932 to 1939. After that, Anna received no more letters from Lisi.

Seventy years later, 15 of Lisi's letters were found in a chocolate box in my brother's basement in Alberta; they are now in the archives at York University, Toronto. Iiris Pursiainen, who lives near Bristol, England, has translated their ribbons of words – without punctuation or capital letters to break them into sentences and paragraphs – from Finnish into English. The letters have been published in *Lines from Karelia* (Arrowhead Press, 2011), a pamphlet which also contains historical photographs and a few poems from *Finns and Amazons*.

Poems in the rest of this book follow a trail – through languages, dark histories, family reticence – which I hoped would lead toward my grandma's lost sister Lisi. When she and her husband Eino migrated to Soviet Karelia, they lived initially in Uhtua (now called Kalevala, the name of Lönnrot's Finnish folk epic) but Lisi's first surviving letter is from a lumber camp in the far north. Lisi and Eino then moved to Karelia's capital – Petrozavodsk in Russian, Petroskoi in Finnish – which had a significant population of Finnish speakers and lively cultural activities including music, theatre, cinema, dancing and gymnastics, as well as political meetings and Russian classes. Both worked at the massive ski factory, and Eino eventually worked as an actor in the Finnish People's National Theatre, which still performs plays in Finnish.

I have been to Finland several times, but my search for Lisi took me to Russia for the first time in 2010. In Petrozavodsk my husband and I were warmly welcomed by my 'stepkin' Anatoly and Nina Shishkin. Anatoly is the stepson of Eino, who had been imprisoned for ten years in the Gulag in Siberia. After his release Eino married Anatoly's mother and the family moved to Petrozavodsk in the late 1950s.

To this day, no one knows what happened to my strong and fearless ancestor, Lisi Mäntysaari Hilberg Hirvonen.

Nancy Mattson 2012

Acknowledgements

Some of these poems, or versions, appeared in print in *THE SHOp, Long Poem Magazine, Acumen, Entailing Happiness* (a festschrift for Robert Vas Dias, Infinity Press, 2010), and *Cardinal Points* 3 (also online at http://www.stosvet.net/12/mattson/index.html). Others were online at *Morphrog*, http://www.morphrog.com; *Tuesday Poem*, http://tuesdaypoem.blogspot.com/2010/10/compasses-triptych-by-nancy-mattson.html; *FinNALA Newsletter* 2 (1&2), 2008, www.finnala.com; and *London Grip*, www.londongrip.co.uk. Thanks to all the editors involved.

Four poems and all of Lisi Hirvonen's letters, translated by Iiris Pursiainen, were published in *Lines from Karelia*, Arrowhead Press, 2011.

"Written in the Name of Rose" is reprinted from *Writing with Mercury*, Flambard Press, 2006, and "Simultaneity I" from *Take Five '06*, Shoestring Press, 2006.

"Compasses: A Triptych" and "Learning the Letter Щ" were shortlisted for the Second Light competition 2009, judged by Pauline Stainer, and published in *Artemis*.

*

My heartfelt thanks to all who have been involved in this book. My nieces, Allison and Danielle Mattson, uncovered Lisi's letters in their family basement. The letters are now at York University, Toronto, Clara Thomas Archives and Special Collections, where Suzanne Dubeau is assistant head; see Varpu Lindström fonds, F0558, Nancy Mattson collection of original letters, 2009-025/042(12). Iiris Pursiainen (BA Honours, DipTrans, MCIL) translated Lisi's letters from Finnish.

John Kouhia, Marjut Nieminen, Kerttu Härkönen, Varpu Lindström, Samira Saramo, Alexey Golubev, Markku Kangaspuro, Elena McNeilly, Simon Geoghegan, Robert Chandler and Anatoly and Nina Shishkin have been cross-cultural guides, friends and much more.

Leona Gom, Robert Chandler, Graham Claydon and Mike Bartholomew-Biggs read the manuscript and made invaluable editorial suggestions; Carol Hughes, Margaret Hollingsworth, Paul Richards, John Roe, Jenny Taylor and Katherine Venn commented incisively on individual poems.

Several of these poems were drafted during my fellowship at Hawthornden Castle International Retreat for Writers; thanks to my co-fellows Jeanette, Daniel, Emily and Donal, administrator Jacob Larsen and the director, Drue Heinz. Thanks also to Cyndy Lumley, Graham Claydon, and Tom and Georgie Adams for providing other places for writing and reflection.

Without the love, support, encouragement, patience and literary sensitivity of my husband, Mike Bartholomew-Biggs, I could never have completed this book. Thank you, soulmate.

Nancy Mattson 2012

Cover painting:
"Sisters of Rural Quebec" [1930] by Prudence Heward.
By courtesy of Art Gallery of Windsor, Ontario, Canada.

I

BACK TO THE AVANT-GARDE

SIMULTANEITY I

That moment in a gallery
when a painting beckons you
to enter   it   unlocks
the door to a hidden parlour

like

that moment in a room of strangers
when a therapist says, 'Find your family
without opening your mouth' and you do
find your father and he tucks your hand
in the woollen crook of his arm
inviting you along to search
for your mother and brother

at

that moment in a garden
when a spider flings a thread
that lands and sticks a yard away
four bricks down the wall
seven bricks right of the gate
and from that single filament
a universe of air and spit is woven

around

that moment in Paris
when 1909 flung itself
outward a century and caught me
in Sonia Delaunay's painted web
that captured a Finnish girl
defiant   surprised   wary   obedient

like

that moment I opened
the door to Sonia's studio
and caught her committing
my great-aunt Lisi to canvas

LA JEUNE FINLANDAISE, 1909

After a painting by Sonia Terk Delaunay

1. Yes, she was a village girl, Karelian,
her mother a laundress.
I supervised the local staff
at the Terks' summer *dacha*
on the shore of Lake Ladoga.
I made sure the servants' children
were never heard, only seen.

Sonia, out sketching, caught the girl
threading flowers in a willow fence,
singing some local folk song.
Sonia wanted the words
but I didn't catch them all –
something about a maid from Kaleva
with shoes and fingers, a waist
wrapped up in grass and gold,
silver and sand,
singing honey and peas,
breaking stones like eggs –
that sort of simple stuff
these people go on about.

Sonia wanted the girl
as a model, I told the poor thing,
'Come inside the big house,
your mother won't be cross,
the lady needs you to hold still
very still on this big arm chair.'

Sonia gave her a glass of cool sun tea,
some madeleines, propped her up
on two embroidered cushions,
arranged her white dress – surprisingly clean –
over her knees, chatted in kitchen Russian.
The girl didn't know.

I taught Sonia how to say *hyvä tyttö* –
that means good girl –
and the little thing brightened up
like a proper sunbeam, said *kiitos* –
that's their word for thanks.

The girl treasures an oil sketch Sonia gave her,
but only the real painting is worth anything.
Even I know that.
No, she never painted me.

2. In my Paris studio, I prop up
my sketches of that Karelian girl

remember the colours
of all those northern summers

all those white nights
when the sun never set over Ladoga

I edge and fill the straight body
with summer, slanted light

humming golden grass
singing silver grass

I shade the flat face
with lake-and-forest deeps

paint the thin arms
and elbows to not quite cover

the thimble breasts
under the muslin bodice

SONIA VISITS LE MUSÉE DE CLUNY

A whiff of damp wool
takes me back to bog and mulch,
the hunt for mushrooms in Russian forests.

A hinge is whining like a distant mosquito,
my arms itch at the thought of welts.

These medieval tapestries are thick with life
as any wilderness, yet how controlled.

I thread myself into the panels,
unpick the unicorn, stitch in the elk
I saw in Karelia, that wonderful beast.

I weave his padded nose, soft as moss,
his dewlap, a dusting rag.

He sniffs strawberries in a clearing
beyond the slurp of dank swamps,

bows to me when I invite him
to settle his shanks beside my chair,

listens to my song until his fur lies smooth
as a stretched canvas for my dabs of paint,
admires himself in my mirror:

his noble hump,
his horns like velvet hands,
his muscular legs and flanks.

His upper lip, loose, ladles
the last berries from my palm.
I shoo him off, go back to my studio.

SONIA'S QUILT

Sonia was no one's muse and no one's fool
but her table always had room
for artists, poets, impresarios, especially those
from Moscow, Kiev, St Petersburg.

No one in Paris could match
the deep pink of her soup,
the yellow of her lemon soufflé,
the white of her poached sole.

She served them wine, designed their books,
their togs and frocks with colour and zing,
torque and zang, hooked them up
with dealers, invited them as partners

to the Paris do-si-do and waltz:
En dedans, come pirouette,
en face, en l'air, come tango swirl
up and around the Eiffel's skirts.

There go the Delaunays now:
see them cut a dash at the Bal Bullier,
look at their art of dancers, rugby players,
aeroplanes, city lights and trains.

They devised a word for all this making,
a grammarless word, *simultané*,
for nothing's ever made alone –
lives and scarves, theories, cards and songs,

discs and planes of colour everywhere,
inside houses, on shopfronts and signs,
not only on easels and walls
where buyers buy and gallery goers go.

Back at home their son toddled and babbled
dada to Robert, *zauma-mère* to Sonia,
slept like a bear cub under the quilt she made,
a mother's gift. Let others call it cubist.

PENSION, RUE MADAME, 1912

Where is Hope? In the dining room
with Love and her governess Adelaide.
Madame Jeanne is serving buckwheat *kasha*
with a melting eye of butter, smiles
of clover honey and a lick of *smetana*.
Paris has a Moscow bite today: even this pair
of Russian women need extra winter padding.
They're meeting Maurice Denis, he'll be glad
if they join his studio, Alexandra says,
but modern women decide for themselves.

Wisdom is taking a bath. She'll be glad
of the *banya* back home: a cast iron tub,
even with flourishes of hot and cold
from elegant spigots, is no substitute
for wood, fire, steam, stone, twigs of birch
to cleanse the skin. Faith is lying down
with a headache. She dreads the journey
back to Moscow, nights in a stuffy couchette.
No matter what Alexandra says, Paris tutors
have no more wisdom for Sofia,
no more faith in art to offer Vera.

Lodgers: Nadezhda ('Hope') Udaltsova; Liubov ('Love') Popova;
Sofia ('Wisdom') Karetnikova; Vera ('Faith') Pestel; Alexandra Exter.
kasha: porridge; *smetana:* sour cream; *banya*: Russian steam bath

KITCHEN, 1912

After a painting by Nadezhda Udaltsova

My first model in a Paris studio was a man
with a feathered headdress and painted skin
stone-still against a backdrop all in reds.
I saw his tomahawk and ran away

to a studio more suitable
where I could sharpen cubist points,
make analyses of angles,
revel in severities.

But the moment I walked into Sonia's kitchen
I found a space to couple art and hunger:
not the romance of cuisine
not the erotics of violins and odalisques
but the sharpness of knives
the beauty of grids on measuring cups
a way of making icons of appliances.

A modern room
where water flowed mercury-white
        from crescent moons of chromium faucets
where the enamel stove shimmered
        with alizarin spatters of beet juice.

An old room
where copper pots curved into spice jars
        wine bottles spun among platters and cups
where stalks of oregano and thyme, filigree and tough,
        hung from the rafters, brushing against
        wheels of hardtack on wooden axles.

While I sketched
Sonia was slicing apples,
weighing manifestos on her scales,
telling me the gossip and news
of Marc, Guillaume, Pablo, Juan, the Steins,
washing gouache from her son's hands.

I drew it all in. Everything.

Over sweet, muscular tea
in porcelain cups of cobalt lace
Sonia unfolded her book design for Blaise.
He would take no persuading after *tarte tatin*
to recite his newest poem, *La Prose du Transsibérien.*

KITCHEN, 2005

An arm's length all around
        no matter where I spin:
everything's at my fingertips.

Too small for a broomstick to wheedle
        crumbs from corners without toppling
glass jars, whacking cupboard doors.

No fan above the hob absorbs
        potato steam or bacon smoke
but there is music: Shostakovich

on the windowsill radio, preludes and fugues.
        And eye-level light: fluorescent tube
a cubit long, elbow to palm. White

poison powder inside a glass wand.
        My rubber gloves detach it from its metal cradle,
degrease it tenderly with Kitchen Witch.

Tonight is duck the butcher's boned,
        stuffed, trussed. Oiled and salted, it
settles reconstructed on a willow platter.

All the Kitchen Devils face left,
        their points ascending in a magnetized line:
paring knives to slicers, choppers, carvers, cleaver.

A Russian icon hangs above the knives
        declaring its corner beautiful. Our Lady
holds her child in the crook of her arm.

Her parallel fingers barely touch
        his saffron skirt, he clutches a scroll,
waves hello, holds me with his eyes.

She gazes past me through the window,
  sun at her throat, stars on her midnight robe.
Everything's at her fingertips.

Our Lady of Grains and Pulses.
  Our Lady of Electricity.
Our Lady of the Gin Bottle.

HOW TO IDENTIFY AN AMAZON

'What is a sparrow? A nightingale that has graduated from the conservatory.'

– Nadezhda Udaltsova, 1907

Looks like a sparrow
sings like a nightingale

Looks like an archer
paints like a donkey's tail

White as a laundress
scarlet as Salomé

Smooth as a Platonist
common as clay

HOW TO REMEMBER SEVEN AMAZONS

Does	Delaunay
Every	Exter
Good	Goncharova
Russian	Rozanova
Painter	Popova
Stay	Stepanova
Unhurt	Udaltsova

BOXERS AT AN EXHIBITION

The Last Futurist Exhibition, Petrograd 1915

In the materialist corner
we have Tatlin the slapdash
wearing red constructivist shorts.

And in the spiritual corner
Malevich the meticulous
in black suprematist silks.

It's a bare-knuckle fight
in a makeshift gallery
where theories bounce
off corners
where icons once hung
manifestos face off chin to chin
the crowd is baying for blood on canvas.

Odds are even, they square off:
Vladimir Tatlin, tall and stringy
rooster on barbed wire,
he's starved himself for weeks
living on paint fumes and sawdust
but his timing's all shot,
he's cock-eyed with jealousy.

Kasimir Malevich, seven years older
bulky as a *boyar*, seven years better
at baiting and besting,
swings his ego at the heavens
with infinite confidence.
His tongue takes off
like a flock of albino pheasants
screeching the merits of pure spirit
but his temper burns holes
in his own manifestos.

Tatlin, his arms loose in their sockets,
throws a left-jabble-dart at the giant and crows,
'Where's your social utility now, Kas?'
then a right-hook-a-took and jeer:
'Hey old man, how about a square black eye
in the far corner of your face?'

Malevich doesn't flinch:
powerful as a grizzly
he sweeps Tatlin to the floor
with one blow, the crowd roars,
Tatlin struggles upward,
tightens his ankles,
locates his feet.

No one dares to referee
until a swish of silk and perfume
glides between rooster and bear:
yes, it's Alexandra Exter, she
prises them apart. The crowd boos
but her oxblood pumps claim the floor
with a blinding shine. Her bias-cut dress,
its black-and-white stripes a danger flag
rippling over torso and hips, slices off
all arguments at the knees.

When she declares
the bout over, it's over;
the exhibition closed, it closes.

BOXING RING

four corners
all red, none
beautiful

SHROVETIDE

After a painting by Pavel Filonov, 1913-14

Fuck eclipses, they're gone too fast
nothing to endure, we just run outside
for some oohs and aahs, the moon
pulls a black curtain over the sun)))
                    (((count 1 and 2 and 3 and
ka-bam the bully sun pops out and smacks us
right between the eyes – we see stars for hours

North of 60, winter plays a long hard game of hide the sun
that ravenous bugger winter, miserable hog of a season
chews at the sun for months, swallows it bones and all
burps and farts like a bear who's had his fill
leaving nothing for us: light-starved, sun-hungry
ready to kill the dark with any weapon

By the day before Lent we're wanting the sun so bad
we bare our shivering arses at that coward sickle moon
squinting behind a smear that tries to play at twilight
but it's no different from a day-long blotch

Enough's enough: we grab our crowbars and hammers
pull our wagon wheels off their axles, set them on fire
shove those blazing hoops down the kids' sliding hill
and cheer on our glory-suns racketing down the slope

When the hill starts losing its curve, like it always does
we know flat ground will win its victory over our suns
    do we know their fate, hell yes
    do we give a damn, hell no
we holler even louder when the wheels start losing their nerve
wobble into death-clatters, plop themselves down
their spokes sizzling through the snowcrust
melting charcoal lines between giant pie-wedges
like the fox-and-geese games our kids play in the snow
with blackened bootprints – and the bastard fox always wins

VICTORY OVER THE SUN

First performed in St Petersburg, December 1913

Come to Luna Park and watch us kill the sun!
Olga's posters hit the city between the eyes
on kiosk walls and pavement bannerboards
her lightning-grease-on-stone lines
her jagged shapes that froze the sneer
of a fast-angled man with a pointed beard.

She drew his eyes as a narrow blaze
a top hat slanting off his head
in howls of snow at midnight.
She crayoned him racing in tails
a biplane chasing him – one last leap
and he'd cheat the frame.
His arm cradled a crystal globe
his fingertips threw letters adrift
free of the printer's rack

ФУТУР ТЕАТР

I can almost hear
his come-on whistle
foooo for ФУ
tooor for ТУР
Come to my opera word dance!
Ride my musical rocket art!

A storm of futurist snow
swirled in his glass belly
Olga's belly, everybody's belly
that winter night at Luna Park
the last month of the last year
before the war to end all wars.

ФУТУР ТЕАТР – 'future theatre'

VICTORY SUN LOOP

Estorick Gallery, 2007

Like the last two children on a beach
waiting for the curtain to open, puppets to dance
before the fairground shuts and the sun drowns

we are the last two adults in a London gallery
aligned on a bench in the crosshairs of time and space

We are the conjuring tricks of Russian futurists come true
eager for a video that loops around eternity in 45-minute orbits:
Victory over the Sun will shoot through the centuries any time now

*Is this St Petersburg 1913 this is Los Angeles 1983 is
this London 2007 this is St Petersburg 1913 is this Los
Angeles 1983 this is London 2007 is this St Angeles
2013 this is Los Petersburg 2083 is this Londangeles
2107 this is*

I am 21st century woman who flew
from Canada in a 747 that chewed up
Greenland like a bear crushing fish

I am Futurist Woman, called to embody
the dreams of Malevich and Matyushin

You are 21st century man who flew
from Peru in an Airbus that swallowed
the Amazon like a bottle of fizzy pop

You are Futurist Man, called to incarnate
the visions of Khlebnikov and Kruchenykh

We say hello in foreign accents, point our eyes
at the flickering screen, a neutral space between us
clamp on our earphones, brace ourselves for lift-off

PARACHUTE LINES

USSR in Construction, Issue 12, 1935 (displayed at Tate Modern, London, 2008)

A faded paper parachute, cheap and green
pops out from the recto page of a Soviet magazine.

Ink lines connect parachute folds to the photograph:
a body in harness, boot-tips on black-and-white grass.

Face against the glass box, I squint at each word:
'A man's life depends on each fold and cord.'

A woman's too: her body strapped up
to a bubble of silk, she must let herself drop.

The tiniest error, say an imperceptible rip
in the cloth or a cord that tangles or knots

and the self slips into the ellipses
between countdown and dot dot dot.

Katia grins, verso, as a Komsomol pilot clamps
the parachute to her back and growls, 'Why laugh?'

A young pioneer's smile is a blizzard of white.
Her happy teeth radiate beams of electric light.

He reaches a high glide, idles the engine, signals.
She jumps of her own free will into a chasm

that freezes her lungs she swallows the wind
gulps a merry whistle pulls the ripcord and ...

Caught in the lens, Katia, you will always shine.
Did you survive, become a toothless grin?

A DREAM OF 33 LETTERS

The poet known as K
dreamed his own alphabet
with twenty metal letters
eleven glass
one liquid
and one
mute
that waited
while thought
slipped between two sounds
into that space between
irony and raindrop

Eleven glass

K took the floor
at the Stray Dog Café
behind eleven glasses
with eleven levels of vodka
pinged a scale of eleven notes
with a rapier tip:
sharp, flat and natural
his glass correlatives for vowels

One note opened the throat
a second made the neck into an echo room
three released the skull from spine
four filled lungs with thundering
five: a gannet, gravity's guillotine

We lost count:
other letters trapped cloud and window
the eye of an animal unblinking
or the way a gait shouts out a person's name

The last was the fire vowel
the one you tighten lips around
to blow and blow on coals
and jump them into flame

One liquid

For an encore
K closed his eyes
and sang a single letter
liquid, monosonic
every sea and river on his tongue
the ebb and flow of tides in our ears

Our hero

We held him on our shoulders
his head above our heads:
K for Khlebnikov
K for King of Time
K for President of Planet Earth
he showed us how to break up
syntax and memories
devise utopian languages

K went astray

We never got to hear
the twenty metal letters that he promised us

the ones he scooped and sieved from rivers
the ones he dug by hand from dirt and stones

He piled up the shiny ones until
they crowded in on his bone-house:

clots of gold and silver
settled in his chest

As mercury oozes from cinnabar
so his sweat became poison

his body a target for lead
moulded into bullets

alkaline letters clicked against his teeth
narrowed his vocal cords, hardened his tongue

noble labials rusted and reeked in his mouth
base gutturals fused into alloys

bronze and brass diphthongs
gave him the chills and stutters

Latterly his frontal lobes crumbled
into islands of forgetfulness

archipelagoes
of phlogiston

One mute

We mourn our poet
Khlebnikov, last seen

wandering unmetalled roads
burning fingerposts for firewood

COMPASSES: A TRIPTYCH

1. Blake drew Newton naked, every muscle
    tense, seated on a rock, hunched over
    the paper world unscrolling at his feet,
    inscribing limits with his compasses
    like God in Milton's paradise.

2. Rodchenko photographs his wife,
    Stepanova, working at her table,
    a pair of compasses in one hand,
    thumb and forefinger twirling the pivot,
    eyes intent on the interlocking spheres
    of her textile design. The universe
    is new from skin to sky. Hand-rolled,
    a cigarette rests on her bottom lip.
    The ash drops, she smiles and blows it away.
    Seed fluff, time flake, off to the past.

    This is no lady painter of aquarelles,
    she's a maid's daughter, Varvara Stepanova,
    calls herself 'Varst' and she can do anything:
    boil pitch or potatoes, build sets for plays,
    shoot billiards, dance tangos, make *zaum*
    poems in syllables, grunts and blobs of paint.
    Varst is sewing canvas overalls,
    her fingertips tough as thimbles. Bites the needle,
    spits a smoke ring through its eye, pulls
    a thread into a V, cuts and knots it.

    Varst sneers at fine art,
    slaps the heads off chrysanthemums,
    uses her brain like a weapon, wages war
    on the object, publishes manifestos, critiques
    all 'isms' and the artists who deliver them,
    writes in her journal with a steel nib,
    nails their quirks and egos.

Rodchenko snaps their circle in groups
and singles, but his wife is his favourite
subject. Never object. She gazes away
from the lens as she points a blade,
arm-length, at six of her collages.

Her self-portrait mocks the easel: forehead
a cross-hatch in blue paint, mouth a scowl
of black X's. She caricatures herself,
her husband too, clowns
with elbows and pantaloons.

3. Never since John Donne has it been so true
as it is with this pair who stride with equal steps:
If they be two, they are two so
as stiff twin compasses are two.

POPOVA'S TURN

After she rejected canvas and easel
Popova turned to plywood, drew
her fingers over its raw patterns,
felt its rhythms, its ad-lib
percussion with soft brushes.

She let the body of wood show through
            deliberate spots of weathered paint:
red grains of cedar still whisper
            where polygons intersect,
the ochres of wide-eyed pine still feather
            the edges of her diagonals.

When the word *sdvig* snuck in between
brush and board, tongue and teeth,
like a laundress at the tsar's ball,
Popova welcomed the shift:
'Hello figure, meet ground,
you have a lot in common.'

Popova learned to be a comrade,
taught at *Vkhutemas* –
heavy clunking acronym
for Studios of Higher Art
and Technical Mastery.

She and Varst grew close as sisters,
shared their compasses and scissors,
drew clothing designs for workers,
hammed it up for Rodchenko's camera,
grinned at the future free of wrinkles.

‘Away with privilege,’ Popova laughed,
threw hers off, committed her hands and radical heart
to propaganda posters, costumes, crockery,
book covers, stage sets, children’s puppets.

But fever’s brush crept in,
painting her son’s body scarlet,
then hers. Stopped her in her prime
at 35. Bodies are not wood but they burn.

The year was 1924. The nights were short.

Popova’s circle of friends wobbled,
mourned, shifted, carried on,
gathered a body of her work
to exhibit in her memory.

Somebody ordered
the body of Lenin
mummified for followers.

The century has turned. Perestroika Roolz
OK. Adam and Eve and Pinch Me
go down to the mausoleum, join the queues
to see if Lenin’s corpse is real.

sdvig: shift, displacement, dislocation

II

LOSS

WHAT CAN BE TRANSLATED

Translation squeezes meaning out of blood,
reduces it to spots of weathered paint
on cedar scraps abandoned in a shed.

Translation plasters over nail-stumps, cracks,
holes. But surfaces are all I have to guide me.
A door is not a tree though both are wood.

Translation flattens nuance into cliché,
peels off layers of stone to reveal only
shadows of fish that once had beating hearts.

Words have no flesh to feed me but I need at least
their traces in languages that touch me.
Skeleton memories. Chalk in my bones.

THREE MILES EACH WAY

'After vile ago,' she said, 've go take it mail now
maybe one two hours today valking tat place.'

My grandma said 'that' like 'tat.' Her tongue
had the knack of tumbling right along through
tangles of time and grammar, the tags and markers
set down by rules as arbitrary as weeds,
a syntax as necessary as vegetables
behind chicken wire twisted into hexagons.
So she never learned to unpick English tenses.
So she left auxiliaries in overflowing baskets of verbs.
She got her nouns across, the odd root word.
My ear could add enough, ignore the rest,
relax into her sense of simultaneous times.

There was no post office building,
only a neighbour's house three miles away:
a six-mile walk twice a week.
I watched her scoop springwater
from the clear layer above the murk
with a dipper, pour it into a thermos.
I watched her weave rainbows into carry-bags
with balls of dyed string and a crochet hook.
Cold springwater. Dust. Straw hats.
String bags. Cows. Salt licks.
She always let me lick the stamps.
Barbed wire. 'Parppit vyer.'
Ginger snaps. 'Seenseri nappit.'
Some flowers I knew: black-eyed susans,
wild roses. Birds I didn't. She called them
words I can't remember, whistled their tunes.
So she simplified all diphthongs.

'So ve taking cookies tat neighbour talk coffee
get letters maybe Finland papers tat news anyhow.'

LEARNING THE LETTER Щ

I'm checking the ways to say that Cyrillic letter
shaped like a Roman three with a heelspur
or cricket stumps with a ploughshare
to cut beneath the bottom line of text: Щ

One teacher suggests I pay attention
to the double thistle in the gap
scratched between two words
whose start and finish match: Welsh sheep

Another says, listen to the scrape
of the hinge in a folding pushchair
or the mother's voice when her baby's shout
drowns out the bus's brakes: Hush child, we're nearly home

Another wants me to try the sound of steam released
when you touch the pressure cooker valve
the cheery whistle of the sealed vessel
shortening the beet time for borshch: БОРЩ

I remember the steam train
screeching to a stop at the station
delivering everyone's grandmothers, flesh-cheeked
babushka-wrapped against December's   harsh chill

I remember the shooshch
of my grandmother's tongue and teeth
sucking her tea through a sugar cube
telling her stories in Finnish

Hush now, it's the one about her sister
in Soviet Russia, how she barely survived
on watery cabbage soup: ЩИ
but was finally crushed   lost   she

disappeared
the sound is a soft *shchi*
one wave in an ocean of millions
that receded but never returned

WRITTEN IN THE NAME OF ROSE

(i.m. Anna Mäntysaari Mattson, 1890-1983)

If I lose her language I may as well burn
what's left of my grandma – her letters to *Liekki*,
Finnish for 'flame'. That weekly paper

came by mail, rolled up tight from Ontario,
its title set in red, all caps, and every letter
painted with fire that couldn't be banned

in Canada, immigrant heaven. Was she a red,
my grandma Anna? A farm wife in the whitest
clump of church Finns in Saskatchewan?

She had no politics that I could hear
with childish English ears, but oh she could hold
a kitchenful of visitors with stories

longer than the rugs she wove from old clothes
in eloquent symmetrics, wide stripes
in colours to match desire with design.

Her voice had the flex and cadence
of an actor's, but her handwriting,
self-taught, was tense and ink-blotched.

Her letters, never two the same shape or size,
struggled across the page like loosened threads
caught on burrs in underbrush.

Surely her thoughts were not so ragged:
decades of *Liekki* editors were keen
to decipher her scripts, print them in columns.

But why did she use a pseudonym?
'*Nimini on Ruusa,*' she claimed:
'My name is Rose and I can say anything.'

Whatever she wrote, it's all lost to me,
my eyes and ears clogged by the ashes
of Finnish, the only language she really knew.

Boxes of unsorted *Liekki* files
are stacked in the Archives in Ottawa,
her manuscripts among them, I assume.

Back issues on microfilm have numbers
but no index. Chronology's as useless
as English for finding my grandma's words.

Anna kept her articles, signed Ruusa,
tied in twine. They were burned by my aunts,
possibly in the name of tidiness.

HOUSE AND GARDEN TIPS

Show no mercy: everything worn-out or broken
must go to the Twenty-First Century Tidy Tip
Stuff incriminating letters and diaries into the cross-cut
        shredder

Out in the bug-free garden, sanitized without pesticides
kindle the bonfire of twentieth century artefacts with decades
of dead wood, hurl in those chamois skins kept to clean
        windows

Save the secateurs, the spades rehandled by dads
Uproot weeds, plant lilac hedges in leninist manure
Cultivate beds of rhododendrons in rich marxist
        compost

Fill razored holes in photographs with heads that flash too many teeth
Overpaint traitors as trees, ignore misfits of hats to heads
thick necks jammed on thin shoulders: all images can be
        transformed

Draw the steam iron over stalinist wrinkles, cover
sagging sofas of gulag survivors with velvet upholstery
Unpick and restitch the dangling bits of history, or snip them
        clean off

Discard all threadbare ideologies, run the new hoover –
anti-allergenic, ahistorical – over floorboards stripped
of dark varnish, suck up any skeletons of bedbugs or
        dust-mites

Vinegar, salt and cigarette ash will clean fingerprints
from prerevolutionary tables, the only furniture worth saving
Fill cracks in logic with linseed oil, buff that spotty history until
        it glows

GHOST SONGS

A needle of sun is following a crawling thing
along the groove between carpet and skirting board
A spectre is haunting me: my great-aunt Lisi
posed beside a Packard convertible
abandoned by Chicago gangsters
    she stared down in Duluth

My grandmother's ink is dark as the day she scrawled
on the back of a photograph she kept taking
from a chocolate box, passing it from hand to hand:
'This is sister Lisi's picture. *Täs on siskin Lisin kuva* '
I place a jar of primroses beside her photo, sing new words
    to an old Scottish tune:

I knew a soldier, his name was Primrose,
he fought in Burma and he was imprisoned there.
When war was over he wed his sweetheart,
oh how he loved the hills of home.

My great-aunt Lisi was born in Finland
her name was Mäntysaari, quite a moniker,
it means Pine Island, a common wildness,
she left her homeland, married twice.

Her second husband, a tango dancer
his name was Hirvonen, perhaps a devil's name
perhaps an elk-man, no doubt a charmer,
he was an actor in Duluth.

They heard the Red call to old Karelia
where merry worker bees in Soviet factories
shook off their old lives, put on their best smiles,
sang songs of freedom while they toiled.

Lisi, I hear a hum through layers of dead drones
through seventy years of static and flak
a yellowed radio's crackle finds a lost
frequency, your syllables rattle the glass
in my sash window, loosen decades
        of dried putty

The woodlouse I've been watching marches west
over a prairie of carpet, reaches the door as it opens:
'Welcome auntie Lisi, would you like some tea
and honey cake, here's a fragrant posy for you
Settle down in these wicker arms, we'll chat later
        if you can stay'

ONCE HEARD

I sense before hearing
        a thunder soft as babies' snores
lazy as underwater weeds
        drifting beside a rowboat
an idle sort of rumble
        kind of soothing, barely audible
it eases pebbles along foothills
        sending riffs of mountain air
to fill my shallow lungs
        force out the airlessness
heavy as the leather library chairs
        I inhabit week after week
not wanting to read but obsessed
        by memoirs of gulag survivors

My sorrow drips on their pages, smears
        my sleeve when tissues fall apart
I swallow my throat hoarse
        at stories of loyal party workers
families split up, half dragged off
        in the night, comrades gone

Random in every chapter
        thunder scribbles a warning
lightning splashes onto walls
        rain fills the broken necks of vessels

Somewhere in every book
        I hear survivors whisper
'Was that ordinary thunder
        or knuckles of pig-iron?'

PARSING THE ANCESTORS

'A poet's speech begins   a great way off'
- Marina Tsvetaeva, 1923

1. Marina's words

Marina's words   shoot star-clusters
into me   occupy skies without amens
bare emotions that bend horizons

Half-air and half-dark   her images: muscles
taut and strong enough   to force
buffaloes over cliffs   I feel no push

toward intensities   but ancestors
chase me   from exploded coal mines
call me from black holes of Stalinistikia

My speech parts begin   in Finnish forests
where deadwood   shifts and crackles
and all echoes ricochet   *kaikki kaikut*

The nouns and pronouns of my ancestors
hook no articles to their necks
hide their genders under hoods

her-less, him-less   the-less, an-less
they declare humans   half-flesh
half-wonder   changeable as stories

told by northern lights   clear as dirt-road parables
deep in ruts of Russian mud   stories that stick
in Karelian throats   thicken tongues of escapees

to places named by natives of new worlds
Saskatchewan   Kaministiquia
overtaken by underdogs from old worlds

My scythe is sharp against the grain
of politics   my father taught me to wrap stooks
with binder twine and unused noose-ropes

instead of joining crowds that bay for blood
I learned to balance   yokes on horses' necks
take over reins   drive jalopies with stick-shifts

Marina's a far cry from my mother   but I tug
at her comet-skirts   latch onto syllables
that squirt   from buffalo-tit to snake-throat

kaikki kaikut – Finnish for 'all echoes'

2. *Akhmatova's shawl*

I grasp Akhmatova's shawl   hungry for knowledge
though not for bread   demanding 'Were you there?
Can you tell me how my missing ancestor died?'   She says no

poetry can't do that   she is sorry   the killed souls
outnumber the galaxies   she tells me
all I can do is search the poles   snatch glimpses

of possible facts   in the timed shadows
of eclipses   until the glare of truth bursts
from behind the moon   smacks me face-on

She tells me to wear protective goggles
but all I have is Kodak negatives   snuck from a tin box
that fail to stop the sun   from burning retinas

3. Blaise's cigarette

The train stops but no one gets off   the station has no name
only a number on the platform signs   men with holsters demand our passports
but there's Blaise   I reach for his right hand   it's not there

he lost it in the war in 1915   his left hand rolls a fag   strikes a match
I inhale the side-smoke   Am I there yet?   No, he says I'm too late
for the agit-prop train the futurists painted   I've missed the Trans-Siberian

from New York to Vladivostok   My father rode the rails in the dirty '30s
jumped on at Moosomin   the Canadian Pacific no longer stops there
but all is not lost   the Vancouver-Helsinki track via Head-Smashed-In-

Buffalo-Jump runs straight through my head   I hear a lost calf bleating
Blaise listens   his ash falls   he assures me the Finland Station still floats
on St Petersburg fens   city of palaces built on swamps and bones

4. Museums of Confusion

I'm the one who mixes up   cards from any deck
shuffles Russian clubs for *durak*   with Italian cups
for *scopa*   replaces one-eyed jacks with red queens

I always get long wooden things   mixed up
hit balls with cribbage boards   stick matches
as counters in canoe paddles pierced with holes

can't tell a millionaire's poker chips   from shavings
that fly from a carpenter's chisel   or a barber's razor
I spin bicycle spokes   instead of roulette wheels   and lose

I'm the one who confuses   languages and blood
demands answers   from desks and pews
marital beds   mug-shots of ancestors

since family women burned   family letters
I'm the one who altogether refuses Marx
but has an ignorant soft spot for Trotsky

just because an old friend and mentor
once lamented   his ice-pick death in Mexico
I'm the one who bought Lenin memorabilia

from a Tampere museum   souvenir matches
with mini-Lenins   in multiple smug serenities
smiling smiling   from the safety flaps of hell

pencils made in China with misspellings
of his surname in Cyrillics   gum erasers
that gradually reduce his head   to crumbs

AMAZON, MUSE OF LOSS

I have found your traces in a sandstone cave
    the colour of faded blood
and in a cabin, hidden under floorboards
    bone broth in your torso notches
I have seen your painted images
    on cliff faces and postcards
your right breast carved off
    for ease of archery
its scar shaped like a star
    in blue printer's ink
your body tattooed with comets
    feather-stitched in red ochre
an antler tip sliced off, sewn on
    as if a nipple to skin

Your blade of honed steel
    sweeps a path to the river
and I follow you, thirsty
    my water pouch flat as dust
I can hear the swirl of the Esk
    but I fear the crane-people
their screech and grasp
    their stone hammers, bronze beaks
that drill holes in temples

Along the river's edge you show me
    where to find
lost footprints, buried implements
    where to hide
from enemies, outwit them
    write them out
how to spear the salmon
    tickle and scoop the trout
whistle to the otter
    shoot the rapids
slide over stones of doubt

FIELDS OF VISION

'May God us keep / From Single Vision and Newton's sleep.' – William Blake, 1802

1. Be prepared to fail, to unexpect
what gets you in the end.
The kaleidoscope's whirl
is full of empty glitter, the index

to history written in print too small
for anyone's eyes
but God's to read.
The photograph of my lost ancestor on the wall

is cracked and smudged, the one she sent
from the wrong side
of a closed border,
her smile too wide as if to prove she was content

in a country of binoculars, everyone trying
to see the future with one lens
cracked, the other blurred,
both eyes worn dry from never no not crying.

2. My naked eye cannot identify
the baby-fist birds that feed on spilled
grain from the millstone, or wait
on innocent fences for bully crows
to grab and swallow their fill.
Strong binoculars, better than eyes
beyond an arrow's range, can show
the black spot on a buzzard's wings,
its tailshape and beak, its gender, but not
the species of its swallowed bones,
nor the fate of its egg-laying mate.
Binocular vision blurs at what's close:
pipits, robins and wrens blend
into feathered blobs. Try as I might,
perception shreds to bits.

RIDDLE OF THE ROUBLE

How many apples can it buy,
a bushel, a core or only a seed?
Would I weep if I lost a single coin,
or secretly dribble handfuls
from my pocket as I walked
along Nevsky Prospekt,
despising them for venial sins
of jingle, bulk and worthlessness?

If I pressed one into biscuit dough
would I see the relief of a bearded man,
a maiden's curls or a matron's crown?
Would it hit the ground from a gambler's flip
on a heron's grace or an upturned duck,
the tail or growl of a tiger or bear?
Would laurels and hammers intertwine,
bullets grin at tractor wheels?

If I cross the border to utopia
where roubles cobble the streets
and grow like cabbages in gardens
or caviar in multiplying sturgeon,
will my questions turn to gold?

PICKLOCK

Perched on a twig, the bird in a cage
my cousin painted in a woodland home
I'd dreamed of all my life without belief
is the oriole I glimpsed in a dome
of branches and sky in a wood circling
a lake of perch, he caught two every day
to fry with eggs for breakfast, unlocking
his skiff from the pier with an Abloy key
chained to his belt beside a gutting knife
sharp as homelessness, he whistled the blues
for his father's home lost in the fall of Viipuri
to Russian troops who crept over borders through
forests without doors or keys or padlocks,
say it in Finn: *munalukkot*, egglocks.

NO BROKEN EGGS, NO OMELETTE

1. *Elegy for Humpty Dumpty*

An egg has no waist or legs
all head it is, thin skull at that
one slap with a spoon-butt
and its cheekbone's broken
one crack with a knife-edge
and it's split from brow to blindside
membrane torn, viscera spilled

2. *Over Easy*

As sure as eggs is eggs we soon forget
that shells were ever anything but

crackable steps to boiled, fried
or over easy in sunny kitchens.

I used to count on the wallpaper
hens that never lay – or is it lie?

Grammar and history abandoned,
we cover over lumps, uncertainties

with what we call interior decoration.
Inside darkened rooms, eggs may weep.

Bacteria we never dare to hold a candle to
may silently attack an embryo gone wrong,

a hidden hope to rise above the common scratch.
There never was an ugly egg until the shell exploded.

WARTIME MOTHER

She kept a cigarette tin
of thumb-tattered cards
a closed set of answers
to probes about the past

No ploy could surprise her
no wish or pleading move her
from her place at the yes-no click
her finger poised on the catch

Someone said the world
has seven basic stories:
she told her life in four
with thirteen variations

no jokers or wild cards
to warp the spin off-true
each story told with a deep drag
on a Player's, the ash drooping

She dealt out the plots
so often our eyelids ached
our tongues went cloth
our ears glue

We learned to exist
off-heart, off-mind
whenever the talk
turned to history

Yet she kept a chocolate box
of letters from Karelia
for us to decipher after she'd gone
one way or another

III

LETTERS

HOBO'S BLOOD

It was like leaving Eden for the hope of Eden,
this journey from new world to utopia.

And they had two sons: Cain and Abel.
Blood spilled on no man's land
before the invention of borders.

And a daughter they never mentioned:
every family has one somewhere.

Ours kept changing names: that's what women do.
Take their husband's. Ours had more than one.

And a string of addresses ever since she left
her father's island for a sister's prairie,
a husband's hotel and billiard room.

Buried him in foreign ground, broke away
with a new husband's trunkful of costumes.

Packed her hobo's suitcase with promises and slogans
that ended in sawdust, *nowhere,* in Karelia.

Wonganperä USSR
19 13/10 32

My dear sister greetings again from here we have been hoping for a letter from you but as none has arrived we have been thinking you may not have received ours indeed we wrote to you almost instantly when we arrived we were in Uhtua one month and then came here to Wonganperä point a lumber camp time goes in such a hurry that any direction we go we stay behind building work happens in a great hurry the first buildings were put up one month before we arrived right in the middle of the forest but now we already have restaurant bakery sauna laundry-hut shop warehouse red corner office building and stable completed another five buildings should reach completion in perhaps a pair of weeks we will get to live in new houses a couple of weeks from now the grand scheme is for each family to have a separate room provided only that time can be found to prepare all the spacing between walls at present there are 21 women here and about 100 men and to my knowledge still more are coming I have been busy doing many different duties picking berries cleaning fishes gathering mosses digging up potatoes and many other little jobs indeed what a lot of berries there were we could not preserve any blueberries for the winter because we lacked suitable containers however we have two large wooden vats full of mashed lingonberries and a third one still to come the great plan was to have one thousand five hundred litres but we did not achieve that because such bad weather came with lots of rain even snow and frost but now the weather is nicer

[letter to Anna Mattson from Lisi Hirvonen]

LETTER FROM SOMEWHERE, 1932

In the unmapped centre of the uncut forest
before we came somewhere from Uhtua
happy workers hustled up the first buildings
        in the fourth year of a five-year plan
        time moves so fast whatever our purposes

restaurant sauna laundry-hut bakery shop
warehouse stables office red corner to hang
faces of leaders posters photographs banners
charts to drill this alphabet into our wooden heads
prepare us to work for the common good
        as our leaders so often remind us
        but our plans our wishes our feet go dragging

in a pair of weeks five more buildings perhaps
we will live in new houses the scheme is a grand one
a separate room for each family if only time can be found
to prepare the making-space-between-us-walls
        I hope they hammer fast
        slap the muddy backside of time

21 women live here now about 100 men
more will arrive I believe in carts and wagons
I keep busy with jobs chosen only for me
        and 20 other women life is merry
        the weather is nicer what else to say

berries for picking with fingers and buckets
fishes for cleaning with knives and thumbs
mosses for hands to grasp from the ground
potatoes to raise from the earth in fistfuls
        so many joyful tasks and little duties
        but fate will soon blow in from the north

so many berries no jars to preserve alas
this blueberry heaven in rows of glass
two wooden vats of lingonberry mash
but the rains came even snow and frost
        our plans to amass a thousand litres
        and five hundred more all gone awash

elokuu the life moon of ripeness has turned
to *syyskuu* the reason moon of cause and effect
now it's *lokakuu* the moon of frozen dirt
soon it will be *marraskuu* we always called it
        moon of death
        our cold fate

elokuu – August, *syyskuu* – September, *lokakuu* – October,
marraskuu – November, *kuu* – moon

SISTER TO SISTER, 1935

So our eldest brother is workless
his wife is suffering illness
indeed it's a life of resistance
sowing hope and reaping rust

Do your girls still have long hair?
I might not even recognize them now.

Our family's stuck in a hard-luck rut
all the seeds our father planted
have grown into a harvest
of targets, rivets, bullets

Is the little one's hair still as white
as the last time I saw her?

It's always the same for the poor
other families are much like ours
indeed we don't float through life
or dance on a field of flower-tips

I plan to have another photo taken:
the one I sent you earlier was blurred.

The old predictions have come true:
the women run on needles
the men walk on knife blades
the children play with hatchets

My sister, I may not see your face again.
Are you connected yet to electricity?

Wonganperä USSR
5 February 1933

... I have still not written to our sister in Finland even though I often intend to I don't suppose she would answer since I am such a red but I plan to write anyway Eino often receives letters from his family there we had freezing weather for a whole week the men got frostbitten cheeks and fingers one day was so cold they couldn't go out in the forest at all we have been thinking of applying for a transfer in spring to a town like Petroskoi this place is a bit too far from the railway and too cold in winter I don't know whether this plan can be fulfilled we have not been too sorry or sad to have left America at least not yet and I hope not in the future either indeed life keeps getting better and better here if only we could just get on with building our project in peace but I know they could attack us at any moment in my opinion though it is too late for them even to try the capitalist countries may have been preparing for war getting their military equipment ready but we have not been asleep or idle either even we women have had shooting practice here I was the best I got 13 points the second got 9 it has been such a long time since I last did any shooting but I did hunt rabbits when I was a little girl and now as a big girl I can still hit a target so I might be hunting the enemy yet I see so that's what they say over there about sending letters from here well I wonder what could be preventing it my evenings tend to be so busy that I haven't got time I have to study I did not learn much Russian we have had only three evenings so far it seems so very difficult to learn but it would be good to know at least a little we put in our applications for nationalisation but have not received anything yet we have not met anyone we know here except for a couple of people whom I had seen in America...

[Lisi Hirvonen]

BELATED ANSWER TO A 1933 LETTER, BELIEVED LOST

As a mouse can slip into a space
thinner than an empty envelope

a letter can nudge a myth aside
put words into another story's pocket

You wrote of your life in a Soviet lumber camp
getting better and better all the time, that line

of Stalin's I think you believed. I'm not surprised
you won the women's shooting competition.

The rabbits you shot as a girl in Finland
were soft targets for a sharp eye.

Did you spy any stray enemies
drifting over the border?

I've crossed that line. Now I walk between
tracks, train my eyes in misdirection,

consider random bullets, false targets
somewhere between not missing America

and the Soviet authorities allowing you
to move to a town closer to the railway.

Call me a capitalist rat. I've inherited your eye.
Call me an enemy hare. Even so we're blood.

As a letter can hide for seven decades
in a space dark as a family rumour

so your story pushes my fear aside
turns the pocket of truth inside out

Petroskoi, 1933

I'll scribble some lines from our new home in Petroskoi we both work at the ski factory time flies too fast when we left Wonkanperä we had snow to the armpits here the ground is clear we planned to go all the way to Leningrad but were a little afraid of language difficulties I must admit I fancied town life again since I lived in towns for so many years now we are in the capital of Karelia it will be a nice town once there are more streets and streetcars to travel around in my job is exactly what I hoped for I always had it in mind to work in a factory at present I work outdoors but that is actually fun as it is warm there are fourteen souls in this tent all with families and a good gang to be with but it is difficult to write when every corner speaks we have already had three entertainment evenings here the theatre group from Uhtua came to perform and films are shown two or three evenings a week we have a radio in one tent when we get to live in rooms there will be several radios and phonographs there is a family from Rouyn Quebec in this tent they know our brother Jacki Gusti and they had travelled from Finland with our brother Iisakki one of the lads has already gotten himself a Karelian muija-missus well young men really don't waste time do they we have joined the Mobriin Oso as well as the workers' union and the gymnastics club there sure is plenty to do here also political circle meetings a couple of evenings a week ...*

*International Workers Aid Society, known colloquially by its Russian acronym, MOPR, established in 1922 in response to a Comintern directive to render material and moral aid to all captives of capitalism in prison

Written on the back of 1933 playbill from the People's National Theatre:

We went to see this play A Million Saints it was a really good comedy set in New York and the Vatican's castle rooms sister Sanna wrote that she is on a local authority farm in Finland I suppose conditions are not so great there either Fiija said she has not received letters from any relatives for more than a year now and was really surprised that we have come here ...

[Lisi Hirvonen]

SCRIBBLES FROM PETROSKOI, 1933

Scribble scribble scribble, *voi voi voi*
we have a new home in Petroskoi
it will be a nice town once we have more streets
and streetcars to travel around in

But it's better than the forest up at Wonkanperä
so far from the railway and snow to our armpits
our plan was to travel by train through to Leningrad
but the Russian language worried us a bit

Time goes flying by when you work work work
both of us work right now at the ski factory
it was always my hope to work in a factory
I admit we're outdoors now but the weather is warm

It will be a nice place when we get to live in rooms
we'll have more than one radio several phonographs too
there are fourteen souls together in this tent
all family people a nice gang all good fun

I try to find places to write but it's hard to think
with fourteen people here and every corner speaking
there's a small village only eight kilometres away
we go there by ship or boat I've learned to row

We have evenings of entertainment three since we came
two or three weekly films and an orchestra
we listen to the radio dance to the phonograph
a theatrical group came all the way down from Uhtua

One family came from that gold mining town in Quebec
they know our brothers Jacki and Iisakki
one young buck has nabbed a Karelian missus
well these days lads don't waste much time now do they

Busy busy busy idleness leads nowhere
we've already joined the workers' union
and the *Mobriin Oso* to send some help
to all the victims of capitalism in prison

So much to do we attend the gymnastics club
and political circle meetings twice a week
we saw this play 'A Million Saints' hilarious
set in New York City and the Vatican

I guess times aren't so great in Finland either
Sister Sanna has gone to a municipal farm
Sister Fiija has had no family letters for over a year
she was quite surprised we came all the way over here

Say hello to all the souls I know remember to write
good night and all the best scribbled by Eino and Lisi

voi voi voi – tsk tsk tsk; ay-yi-yi

SONG OF THE SHOCK WORKER

In 1935 at 36   I let my body go electric
    shocked it into work that squeezed an extra

dozen minutes out of every hour
    multiple seconds out of every clock-tick.

Who believes arithmetic?   My body flew beyond it.
    For every pair of skis I polished off   I notched

a cross on the window ledge   racked them up
    like pikes in rows   threw myself into cut-short nights

but sleep was full of chinks   the swing of blunt axes
    dead crows hung upside-down   from birch poles

their limp wings   black flags on fences
    flapping through my dreams.   So I bolted

life onto my workbench   hands hardened by fire
    fingers charming as fish-hooks   with the sprung grace

of ski tips   my thumbs tough as tempered steel.
    My teeth sizzled   as I sharpened skis

sanded them smooth along the grain for swiftness
    left them rough the other way   so skiers never slip

backward.   Backward? I never go there.
    My eyes always press forward   like headlamps

on the car I used to own with Eino in America.
    Let him clamp those wooden strips on his feet

race to other villages through endless trees
    cut lightning trails   through drifted snow.

I'm a worker not a skier.   Smile Lizzie smile,
    grin Lizzie grin! the bosses say

I'll win a prize for sure.   Work is my power:
    the sweet electric therapy   of sweat on skin.

Petroskoi USSR
March 18th 1935

... I have been having a lot of fun in honour of women's day I was awarded a shock worker's prize a trip to Leningrad we were a big gang of 40 women from all over Karelia including 12 Finns we set off on the evening of the 5th and arrived in Leningrad on the 6th we were taken to a tourist hotel then we were taken out on excursions every day everything was very interesting to see and hear we were given running commentaries everywhere we went on the 7th we visited Peter and Paul Fortress and church and Isaac's Church on the 8th we went to a rubber factory they had 36000 workers in three shifts Uritski Palace and Smolny on the 9th Catherine Palace and Alexander Palace one palace actually had 157 rooms in the evening we went to the circus on the 10th it was the art museum in the evening we started the journey back to Petroskoi we had so much fun we were off work and yet we were paid our wages only two days after returning to work I injured my foot and have been off work but it seems to be healing fast the doctor may allow me to go back to work next week ...*

*the actual figure is 1057

[Lisi Hirvonen]

PENCIL AND BLOT

My name is Pencil, *Karandash,*
and I dash around making circles in a ring,
my head a sharpened lead that I grind every night
with my *tochilka* and top with a pointed hat of stiffened stuff.

I do not use my voice. My tongue stays still but my body
writes loops of silliness. I practise like a dancer
but one always tripping over shoes ten sizes too big
like leather canoes, or bumping into a chair he never notices,
a dancer whose trousers insist on falling down,
the crowd loves that, but *Karandash* never exposes
anything but baggy underdrawers in bright yellow silk
with big blue polka-dots. They shout and point
when my red suspenders stretch from Leningrad to Moscow.
They howl when my terrier – his name is Blot, *Klyaksa* –
barks at my ankles, catches a cuff in his teeth and will not let go
as I run the other way, as if I do not know.
Dear *Klyaksa*, he can smell the slices of sausage
I hide in my pockets, he gets one for jumping through a hoop.
They clap when he stands on his hind legs and begs,
sing when he dances the *kalinka*, snap their fingers
to his perfect timing when he cocks his crooked leg,
but they roar like a thousand tigers in a cage
when *Klyaksa* flips himself up and over sideways:
I give him five slices for that. Even a beast needs prizes.

The trick is to keep a straight face when everyone's laughing
as if there's no tomorrow – which there is not.
It is only tonight we are here. Some clowns
paint red greasy frowns like sausages
drooping from the corners of their mouths
but that's too obvious for *Karandash:*
all I need to do is raise my eyebrows, twitch
my thick black moustache and pretend to be alone,
in charge, as if I have no clue what else is going on.

tochilka*: sharpener*

WRITING SPREE, 1935

The spirit of writing letters is truly upon me
like the wind blowing up pages of powdered snow.

Already I've written to Fiija-sister in Finland
that wise old broom who never left her doorstep

and my girlhood friend who moved to Minnesota
that busy little mother with all her on-and-offspring

How's our restless brother who moved back to Saskatchewan?
Does he visit you with his ever-grinning wife,

that nervous hare, is she somewhat calmer now
or has she hopped back into hullabaloo-house?

Have all the Hemmings tied the marriage knot yet
and are the ancient gray-hairs still alive?

Do you still keep in touch with Mary Holmström?
I admit my letters to her remain unwritten.

What about Kalle and Esteri, are they still fighting
the scrub-brush and stones on that old Simpanen place?

I used to correspond with that Amalia
but I haven't gotten round to writing her since

my leather shoes hopped off the Murmansk train
in Petroskoi, where we're building paradise.

MISSING LETTERS

I wrote you a letter
parallel lines
crucial data
new address ~~a friend's~~
our mother kept safe
our little brother and me
I need official stamps
for crossing borders
right right whoops

in two columns
double blocks
clear instructions
where to send the passport
the one she carried to bring
her last children to Canada
lined up in proper order
left right left
I meant left

**

Alone in my room at night
I follow painted footsteps
of tangos and foxtrots
filled-in circles
half-filled circles
my man's legs are gone
my right leg tries
my left leg fails

under a single bulb
on paper diagrams
numbers for bars
for left-leg pivots
for right-leg drags
his body his arms his eyes
to occupy his left-leg air
to draw his right leg back
between my thighs

**

Censors cannot imagine dancing
their minds trained in facts and duplicity
left brains sharp as curved razors
right brains blunt as hammerheads
clever me I scrapped the columns
rewrote my letter in alternate words
on the front of a cut-up ace of spades
and the back of a torn-up theatre playbill

Even a Finn in the pay of the Office
of Rooting Out Spies and Enemies
would be too feeble
to reconstruct my sentences
by putting my pieces of ace-card
and troupe-list back in order
voi voi voi that former friend
or neighbour would say
what nonsense what babble

Maybe you never received
my envelope filled with secret code
I never received the passport
I need to leave this country
maybe your postal service is worse than ours
maybe their system is smarter than mine

POTEMKIN SYMPHONY NO. 37

known as 'The Silent Symphony'

Let this fine orchestra be immortalized
at its final dress rehearsal

let the musicians take their positions on stage
let the strings poise their bows in parallel air

let the brasses push their lips into a ready embouchure
let the woodwinds wet their reeds as water kisses the shore

let the percussion subdue all sound
let the conductor lift his baton

Now, everyone freeze for the photographer. Again. Perfect. Again.
Posterity will be grateful for visible evidence of your talent.

Now, all orchestra members are under arrest. Control, please,
your tongues. Your instruments are to be confiscated. Hand them
to the uniformed officer who will record your names,
ages and occupations in the official log book.
File out through the stage door at the rear of the building.
All concerts are hereby cancelled, the box office closed.
The state has no further need of your music.

PENCIL STUBS

She hoards pencil stubs, files them away
underneath a loosened floorboard
writes facts to her sister on the backs
of cast-off manifestos printed in Cyrillics.

She writes of her husband, dragged away
as labour fodder for a spade gang
one of thousands – who's keeping count
forget it, line them up in rags

call them skin mallets, buckets of bones
for hand-digging the White Sea Canal –
Belomorkanal – a shallow ditch
a couple of hundred kilometres

through permafrost and granite
swamp and springmelt
lined with rottable wood
such a feat of hollow engineering

that the state issued a new cigarette
to honour it, *papirosa*, the same
diameter as a bullet, 7.62 mm:
pop that in your mouth and suck.

Everyone loves a daily hit
of *Belomorkanal* – twenty-five
cheap plugs of high-tar tobacco
in disposable cardboard tubes.

Every puff of smoking pleasure
celebrates tens of thousands
of canal-builders burnt out
thrown away like *papirossi* stubs.

She stares at a shredding poster:
"Canal Army Soldier! The heat of your work
will melt your prison term!" Moistening
her pencil lead through cracked lips

she writes of a daughter, given away
taken away what's the difference
to the camp commander, spermless
and his barren wife in furs.

GODMOTHER

She gave me her daughter
as she killed another cockroach
saying, 'Take her away
as far as Saskatchewan.
Have her baptized Varpu,
she's thin as a willow twig.
Let her be a whisk to brush
a cupboard dustless, sweep away
the godlessness that crushes us.'

I cannot take her daughter
to Canada, but I know a priest
in Moscow. He lives in a secret room
small as a coffin; and I will teach
this girl my grandmother's prayers.
Furs and silks can hide simplicity.

As my grandmother said:

In the land of the blind
the one-eyed jack is king.

In the land of the footless
the limper believes.

In the land of secret police
baptism is invisible.

KITCHEN PERESTROIKA

The classic method, invented before the Bolsheviks,
worked equally well for the Soviets. Peel them raw
or slip off their skins after boiling and dipping
in cold water. Dice their flesh to the same size

peas would be if peas were cubes: potato cubes,
carrot cubes, beet cubes, pickle cubes, swede cubes,
finn cubes, polish cubes, kraut-or-jap-or-ukie cubes,
traitors, jews. They're all the same on the cutting board.

Place them in a clay bowl, cool them in the icebox
to 37.6 degrees, no more no less. As the tongue
of the tsar was tender, so our party leader prefers
nothing too hot or too cold. Mix ingredients well.

Mask identities with mayonnaise. Forget names,
numbers are more precise: vegetable 1, vege 2, veg 3,
4, 5 and so on and so forth, but the total must be odd.
Serve on circular plates in off-centre domes.

This is the joy of salad cubes, our leader's favourite dish,
the relish of reconstruction: vegetable *perestroika*.

In Petroskoi
19 July 1939

My dear sister and family Thank you for the letter which I received all the way back in February it was such a pleasure to hear from you I have not been able to answer sooner as I've been busy again with moving house and such I wasn't really sure where I would end up living but I managed to get back to Petroskoi after all and I'm back in the same job as before they do say that variety refreshes I got a place to live with a girl I know so I'm getting on with life again with little cat steps I have not yet asked anywhere about that thing it is hard to think about that so for the moment I'm just planning to see how things go how is everybody over there are all of you well are Emeli and Olga still living with you has Elle written to you how is she managing with her child or has she got married is Esteri still in hospital I often think about you all and miss you dreadfully now that I'm so alone here but that's my fate my mind tells me I should have stayed in Canada instead of wandering off like a hobo I have come to the conclusion that people who spend their whole lives in one place are the happiest and most contented even though I have understood it too late oh well never mind I can't get time back have you had a warm summer it has been really cold here only a few warm days I have not even been for a swim yet we went to the summer park yesterday evening but got so cold that we had to go home there is really nothing there to amuse anyone as old as we are any more although one does hear beautiful music there ...

[Lisi Hirvonen]

PETER'S FACTORY TOWN, 2010

The humble twin of elegant St Petersburg, this town
of factories for skis, chairs, tractors, tanks and tools
was built to forge swamp iron into shot and cannon.

These weary barracks of Petrozavodsk were once the new
wooden buildings of Petroskoi hammered up behind old
neoclassical walls; now the nails are coming loose.

Post-soviet workers are fixing the mouldings
of crumbling façades, floating fresh plaster
and pastel paints over graffiti that scold

Putin and Medvedev for crimes and disasters
unknown to me. Though I can decipher names
in Cyrillics, political phrases zoom right past me.

I'm here for the remnants of Finns who came
to build homes, work in factories, offer their skills
and brains, their hearts and hands to flames

that would burn the capitalist past to ashes, fulfil
the promises of Stalin that life was bound
to get better. My great-aunt Lisi swallowed the pills

she believed were panaceas, though she found
they melted to nothing in her mouth
except for the bitterness she spat on the ground

when no one was looking. She was loth
to admit the last nine years had been a hoax
but in her final letter, loneliness wrote the truth:

'I've understood too late, nothing turns back clocks.
Not much in this place can amuse someone of forty,
although one still hears beautiful music now and then.'

STASH

I hide them away in a tin box
with a hinge, a sailor on the lid
I read them all again and again
in order, backward, sometimes

shuffle them or shut my eyes
pick a single leaf at random
like a raffle ticket from a basket
to catch myself by surprise

Remember the cat we had
that pounced at its own shadow
on the wall or dust in the light
for lack of a fresh mouse?

Your letters never become stale
but I handle them so much
my fingers can read them
their words are in my bones

their paper scarified along the folds
air threaded between words
I know so well I recite them
as I scrub sheets on the washboard

rub my knuckles against its ribs
wishes against facts, your words

as intimate as clothes
softened by years of washing
as tough as sinews
holding my body tight

IV

LEGACY

Petroskoi USSR 18 March 1935

... it really would be good to come for a visit over there but I don't know whether we'll ever see each other again we have not made a decision yet regarding that matter I wrote to you about I guess some letters have gone astray you must have 'lost-on-the-road spirits' over there I did not even receive the one in which you had sent some paper do you have electric lights yet are times still bad over there has there been any improvement at all things just keep on getting better over here it is already 11 o'clock I must go to sleep and continue tomorrow ...

USSR Karjala 17 January 1939

... I've been working here at the forest punkt for just over three months now variety refreshes as the saying goes I guess this is one way of making time pass but we don't know where we might end up in future I don't know what would be for the best I have a lot to write about but I don't seem to know how to do it any more because I write so rarely any minute now I'm going to turn illiterate I would like to ask you something maybe you can guess could you ask our brothers Jacki and Eemeli and John's wife Lisi she has promised she might also take part if this comes to anything at all or what do you think write to me about it ...

[Lisi Hirvonen]

PAPER, TONGUE, STONE

> *'do you see how everything shifts a bit each second*
> *grows simpler, more primitive'* - Eeva-Liisa Manner, 1966

You left me the need to read your letters
ask for help to understand your words
but translation is no simpler than history

In 1939 you wrote to your sister
'I write so rarely any minute now
I'm going to turn illiterate'

Your voice is getting clearer but it 'shifts a bit
each second' between reticence, omission
and your wish to cause no worry to your sister

It isn't getting simpler or, as Eeva-Liisa writes
the comparative of 'simple' – *vaatimattomammaksi*
I can roll its syllables around my tongue and teeth

but settle for something more primitive –
stones on gravel roads, beaches, riverbanks
stones in my palms, words in my pockets

I line them up on windowsills
by pattern, colour, size or shape
load them as cargo in clay boats

white pebbles with tide-softened commas
of clouded glass in greens and blues –
the stories you could not tell

Stones are illiterate, ubiquitous
I asked for meaning, Lisi
and you gave me only

birds with stone throats
trees with stone leaves
your trail gone cold

AT KONDOPOGA, LAKE ONEGA

Factory 1929, Church 1774

So many letters written, propaganda tracts
histories, revisions, red and yellow newspapers

as though the paper mills of Kondopoga
would never stop turning
their walls never stop rusting
their chimneys never stop spewing
ash into Karelian air

as though malodorous liquors, black and brown
would never stop flushing into the mouths
of streams that flow into Onega
vast as an inland sea

So many prayers of Old Believers, hymns chanted
icons painted, loaves and fishes blessed

as though the doors of the wooden Church
of the Dormition of the Mother of God,
Theotokos, would never be locked
none of its priests be killed

Yet it stands tall, its glass eyes
looking west across an inlet
narrow as a pair of fishing nets
where an iron behemoth
blocks the sunset:
Behold, it devours forests
chews them to pulp
exhales Stalinist fumes
into the Virgin's face

A village *baba* leads us up the wooden stairs
turns a forged key in the heavy-bodied door
lifts her skirt over the blackened threshold

The medicinal tang of wood tar
centuries thick
is welcoming as licorice

Grids of light from tiny leaded panes
guide our feet across uneven planks
lead our eyes to icons on log walls

Several are Marys, most with her wise-born
baby on her arm, one with a preborn
adolescent saviour inside her belly-world

White scarves drape the shoulders
of the icons, flowers in vases
scent their painted feet

Beside the doors to the holy of holies
Mary sleeps, budded limbs of gladioli
framing her and her risen son

a baby swaddled in white on his arm
a clutch of saints and angels
crowding around her cold bed

Proud on its headland this church stands
a tree made of trees. When Lisi visited friends
in Kondopoga she couldn't have failed
to notice it but wouldn't have been inclined
to climb its stairs, light a candle or mention it
in a letter. No, she lived and died
somewhere between factory and church

KARELIAN PILLOWS

Tradition stuffs them
with buckwheat on the hard side
duckfeathers on the soft

My hotel pillow in Petrozavodsk
was half-buckshot, half-recycled carpet-tufts
a pair of enemy 'don't-touch-me's in one pouch

Back in London my sheets are sprouting thumbtacks
through burlap interwoven with nettle twine
the duvet fills with gravel, pins me to the mattress

Bedsprings are cedar roots pushing through loam
I wrestle with 'that matter' in Lisi's letters
Even if someone guessed it, nothing could be done

My bedclothes twist, the struggle lasts all night
I wake exhausted, ropes of sleep limp in the light

RED TENTS

Tramping through a northern forest
without a compass or watch
on perhaps the shortest night
I stumbled on a campsite

coals breathing, log benches idle
tent-flaps tied against creatures
tent-walls glowing the soft red
of inner lamplight, canvas-muted

Silhouettes emerged as women's bodies
whispers hardened into shouts to confront me –
  was I a bear, skunk, moose?
then chuckled at my furlessness

I couldn't understand their words
but hunger is bigger than fear
and language matters less than bread offered
or stew reheated on fire rekindled

I watched the stars disappear
in the bottom of my tea mug

This morning they greeted me as trees
I thought I heard the wind say the word Karelia –
  Finnish breath or Russian?
but breezes and leaves know nothing of borders

I heard the songs of open-throated birds
their chests red and proud as the one
the Finns call *punarintasatakieli*
red-breast-a-hundred-tongues

punarintasatakieli – robin

SEEN NOT HEARD

after Reijo Kela's 'Silent People'

their hair is grass
their heads are turf
the silent people who stand in a field
their clothes are old
dresses the dead
no longer need
faded sweaters
shirts outworn

the quiet people
their faces dirt
whose skeletons are wooden crosses
stuck in earth
for time's length
the planted people
without growth

no signs identify
warn or guide
nameless people we wander around
reading undated
cloth epistles
fingering labels
under collars

the harmless people
don't smile or talk
even the reindeer don't knock them over
wide open to touch
they stand their ground
static until the wind fills
sleeves with arms

the cryptic people
a thousand or so
every spring the local youth assemble
charity garments
spades to renew
faces and heads the
snow has melted off
wind has eaten away

never alive
though not unproud
their thoughts are silent letters in foreign words
they slow us down
empty our minds
leaving no tracks
themselves

ON PAIN OF DEATH

I first played it in the dark, on a street of jewellers. Never mind afford or want, she said. Stopped our walking conversation at a window clotted with glitz, the gems so large they hid the chains and clasps of necklaces and bracelets. The needle-and-socket fastenings of brooches. Never mind you can't imagine anything by Cartier on your neck or wrist, pinned to your chest, or wrapped around your waist. The given word is must. The task: to choose, on pain of death, one item in the window you could be caught alive in, wearing.

We play it in galleries, the paintings for sale or not, the artists alive or dead, the gallery a Hermitage, Louvre or the little shop on our street with a scottie dog in the doorway who answers to Duffle. When love has lasted years, when lust is a game we play in public spaces, when even exquisite stuff no longer tempts us to own it. Our tastes in art are chalk and silk. But the game is deadly serious and must be fed with agreement. We take one home, for we do not wish to kill each other through indifference. Today a Morandi print, his small family of bottles and jars arranged in the only pattern we can both, on pain of death, imagine living with.

I play it with a new book of poems, the gift of someone whose judgment I think I trust. A poet lauded and prized. Not to my taste. Dried lutefisk on the tongue. By poem five, I'm ready to chuck it in the Oxfam bin. Correction, donate it. But under the giver's breath an unspoken injunction: on pain of death, find one poem you can treasure. One year I reread Pope, his wit initially a thorn I could not swallow. It took a beloved tutor, deaf and erudite, to drag me into the 18th century, open up Pope like a box of fresh figs in tissue-paper nests, take me up the Thames to Twickenham. Today's task, without a guide: keep on reading or sink without a struggle. Finally, a long poem with an ecological core beyond ego and swagger. Finally, a line for that forest graveyard in Karelia where my great-aunt was not buried. *Isotäti* Lisi. I cross a fence, open a knee scar left by old barbed wire. Stalin's dead and gone, never mind the past my brother says. But I had to go where Lisi chose to go. On pain of death.

TO QUEST IS HUMAN

1. 'Who leaves their home for something that makes sense?'
   my friend who channels Dusty Springfield wonders
   on the road to Rosslyn Chapel. The hopes I had
   for something peaceful, even holy, are squeezed
   by the crowds who come to gape not worship.
   Greedy for coded conspiracies they guzzle
   plonk from plastic cups, believe a man
   who says a grail whose holiness is alien
   was buried in this crypt. The clown face feeds
   a taste for junk, fills them up, they babble
   with the tongues of jelly babies.

   Still, this is only dour Scotland; no one
   follows gurus like the rev. Jim Jones
   whose promise of paradise in Guyana
   ended in galvanized tubs of fizzy pop
   diluted with river water, saccharine
   bubbles flattened with cyanide.

2. It didn't make much sense for me
to follow the ghost of an ancestor
lost in Karelia on the cusp of war.
Did it make sense for her to trust
in a utopia she didn't dream
was poisoned? Her last letter allowed
possible folly, admitted loneliness,
accepted her fate. No signature.
She could have been anyone's kin.
No death certificate, no grave
to visit. The gap of unknowing,
wide as a river. Did she ever see these falls,
the shattered waters of Kivach?

Its legend tells the story of two sisters,
always side by side chatting and laughing,
until the afternoon one fell asleep
and the other wandered off, followed another
channel. The woken sister broke down rocks
and boulders in her frantic search but never
found the lost one. Now she weeps continually:
quick flow above, quiet pool below.

SIMULTANEITY II

That moment in a library
when you find a guidebook
and brush off forty years of dust
inhale the smell of Scottish castle
and suddenly you're in Moscow
fifty years after the revolution

like

that moment in a gallery
when a girl in your pinafore
looks so hard at a painting
that you know you must not
disturb her   but you want to
tap her shoulder   ask her name
ask why she looks exactly like you

at

that moment on a sofa
when you held your rubber doll
in the crook of your arm
and a rubber pilot landed his biplane
on the upholstered runway
beside the ashtray on a pedestal
where your father left his cigarette
when he held the camera very still
and the smoke curled

around

that moment in an e-mail
when your niece says they've found
a chocolate box of letters
in the basement   from Russia
written by Lisi to your grandma
do you know who that Lisi is
and you do   start shaking

SPLICE

that moment in a forest in Karelia
when a man brushes dead leaves from a stone
and you read the letters carved in black granite
ТАМАРА – his Siberian mother, Tamara
ЭИНО – her Finnish husband, Eino
ХИРВОНЕН – you know the surname, Hirvonen
Lisi took it when Eino was her husband
and in your mind you see them
in a newsreel never shown   blink

to

that moment in 1932 when a liner full of Finnish workers from New York lands in Leningrad the gangplank clatters Eino and Lisi are racing hand in hand dockside to pavement to platform they catch the same breath a steam train following the pole star is it really red comrades forward through Karelia

to

that moment in 1934 when Lisi writes that *Eino longs to leave this place* go off to sea to college anywhere her pencil wavers only once in 1935 when she calls him tenderly 'Eikka' his theatre troupe is off again in Uhtua *no point in writing much about that* she says *it's best to forget about that as if it were merely a dream I had*

what about fears   none are written
what about the terror   not one letter
from 1937 is in that chocolate box
you have to go elsewhere for poison

DISAPPEARANCE

has no moment
either it takes forever or it hides

by 1938 she slips in
weather talk
letters-from-home talk
don't-worry-about-me talk

between job talk and
a couple of lines
about him
he's only a surname by then

Hirvonen's living in Petroskoi
with his wife I rarely come across them
it doesn't feel like anything any more
we say hello that's all
one can get used to everything

even the *anything*   buried under *any more*

by 1939 she's been up north again
that old familiar nowhere
but now she's back in Petroskoi
getting on with life in little cat steps
I study every word in her letters   as grandma did
dare to fill some gaps   say

the moment of arrest when
    the NKVD came for Eino
the moment he heard his sentence
    ten years in the Gulag
the moment under the hay moon
    when Lisi's tongue
    touched the glue
    that clogs interrogation

she signed that last letter   *your sister*

her sister   my grandma always left
    a hole when she knitted
    a sock   a mitt   a glove

LISI LEFT

no gravestone   no official papers   no fate
no so-what   no what-else   no more plans
but I stand on this earth   among half-bare trees
shoulder to shoulder   with three who know
her name   and the need
for certainty   blood   disappears

into the moment we plant
on Eino and Tamara's grave
cloth flowers whose colours
would make me sneer
anywhere but here

I declare lilies
orange for Saskatchewan
pronounce roses
pink for Alberta   white for Finland   red for Russia
their fluorescence so bizarre
it embarrasses borders into dissolving

this search ends   *our father*   tumbles unbidden
out of the mouth   *hallowed be thy*   brokenness
releases tears   *on earth as it is*   cuts to the heart
of words gone old and dull   splits them open
to the core of prayer   scraping the throat
one by one   as never before

a hard swallow   a way to breathe
a voice takes words by the tongue
through   *trespass against*
and *thine is the kingdom*

wood never dies   *amen*

NIGHT TRAIN, PETROSKOI TO PETERSBURG

"I haven't been here for seven hundred years,
but nothing has changed." - Anna Akhmatova, Tashkent 1942-44

I haven't been to Petroskoi for seventy years,
the trolley buses are rusted, the tractor factory closed.

I know the numbered limits of forgiveness:
seven times seventy. Not one morsel or scruple more,

not one patch or sliver, scrap or jot or smithereen
do I owe the enemies of my fair-haired ancestors.

The reaper's moon is searching out the platform
for anyone coming late to say farewell.

The almond-eyed attendant in navy serge
checks the tickets, has plenty of time

to smoke and flirt in a pencil skirt,
coarse black pumps that can't stifle glamour,

a neat little cap at an angle, a wink that signals
a leather-jacketed chap she's ready for more.

She's stoked the stove with wood chips, filled
the samovar with water, stacked the tea glasses

beside their filigree holders of faux silver,
folded linens and blankets in all the sleepers.

Like a poet descended from Darwin
moonlighting on a Russian train

perhaps she's watching me as I watch her,
recording the scene for patterns of blood

relatives once or more removed,
prisoners lost and those who survived –

perhaps not the fittest but the luckiest,
the seven times seventy blessed –

the ones born over enemy borders
and those who pulled their shadows

through lapses in barbed wire fence,
gaps between trees and their leaves –

enemies of luck, friends of traitors
locked in cages, sentenced

to five years, ten years, a hundred and forty
or fifty moons to scratch on walls, losing track –

if we are related to all creatures, even spiders in cells,
we are related to those who imprison us,

those we entangle in webs of obligation
broken only ...
                    The full moon escapes the clouds

and here they come, breathless, semi-cousins
who keep their promises, whose blood

runs unshared between us, circulates under
separate skins that touch in reflected light.

They bring food and gifts, one a carving
that fits my palm – a bird in local birch

swinging on a thread in an onion dome
under an orthodox cross in polished brass.

Thank you   *spasiba*   *kiitos paljon*
Nina and Tolya: newborn family, farewell.

DOUBLE

Moscow Tourist Guide, 1967

The girl on page 219, hands on her hips
in the Tretyakov Gallery, wears my school pinafore:
knife-pleats drop straight down from a square yoke.

She's a Soviet girl, her eyes riveted
to a horsewoman ten feet high whose hat
perches on tangles of hazelnut curls.

Her own hair is white, cut short,
razor straight. My mother
was her barber, said hold still.

The girl puzzles out the painting:
black horse pulled up short from a gallop;
the rider's grey organza scarf flying behind

like long dust, a cobweb merging with trees;
her face calm as the painted features
on a porcelain doll. The whole picture

whirls around that oval face:

the horse's eyes loose in their sockets,
nostrils wide as openings to dark caves,
tongue wrestling the bit; a collared whippet

and a lace-and-ringlets girl laughing
on the balcony; a spaniel yapping at the rider,
her skirt a silk waterfall down to the horse's knees.

A story can be spun on random kinship:
that balcony girl grew up to be
the Soviet girl's *baba*. Or delicious fear:

black horse, what big teeth you have,
they could bite through a lady's wrist,
your iron hooves snap off her dolly head.

The dogs tried to warn her. I reach the wall.
History goes so far, then story and wish leap over.
I've never been to Moscow, yet the pinafore girl

on page 219 is my photographic twin,
staring at the painting as I stare at her.
Tretyakov girl, what blood have we in common?

NOTES

La Jeune Finlandaise, 1909 - Sonia Terk Delaunay was born in Ukraine but raised in St Petersburg by a rich uncle who had a dacha on Lake Ladoga in Finnish Karelia. Snippets of folk song are based on phrases in Cantos 20 and 21 of *Kalevala*, trans. Keith Bosley, Oxford University Press, 1989.

Sonia Visits Le Musée de Cluny – The six medieval 'Lady and the Unicorn' tapestries were acquired in 1882 by this Paris museum. Sonia moved to Paris in 1905. The wonderful beast *alces alces* is called *elk* in Europe, *moose* in North America, *losi* (лоси) in Russia, *hirvi* in Finland, *orignaux* in France.

Sonia's Quilt - Bal Bullier – a Paris dance hall and the subject of Sonia's first major painting in 1912-13. *Zaum* is a Russian nonce-word for 'beyond sense', a type of non-rational poetry practised by some avant-garde Russian poets. Sonia's 'Cubist Baby Quilt', 1910 or 1911, is reproduced in many art catalogues and books.

Kitchen, 1912 – Nadezhda Udaltsova wrote in a memoir of her terror at seeing a "red Indian" model in the studio of Maurice Denis. See John E. Bowlt and Matthew Drutt, eds., *Amazons of the Avant-Garde*, London, Royal Academy of Arts, 1999. Sonia and Robert Delaunay's friends included Marc Chagall, Guillaume Apollinaire, Pablo Picasso, Juan Gris, and Gertrude Stein. Blaise Cendrars' poem 'La Prose du Transsibérien' was illustrated by Sonia, interweaving her art and his words. It is a long skinny poem (about 6 feet) folded up accordion style. The plan was to print 150 copies; laid end to end they would have been the same length as the height of the Eiffel Tower. Only about 50 were printed. The British Library purchased a copy in 2007.

Boxers at an Exhibition – Exter's intervention in the fist-fight between Tatlin and Malevich at the 'Last Futurist Exhibition' in Petrograd, 1915, is mentioned by Camilla Gray, *The Russian Experiment in Art 1863-1922,* Thames and Hudson, 1962, rev. 1986.

Shrovetide - The custom of rolling burning wheels down hills during Shrovetide celebrations is mentioned in a note on Pavel Filonov's painting *Shrovetide* reproduced in Yevgena Petrova & Deborah Horowitz, eds., *Origins of the Russian Avant-Garde,* State Russian Museum & Palace Editions, 2003.

Victory over the Sun and **Victory Sun Loop -** The futurist opera *Victory over the Sun* was performed twice in St Petersburg in December 1913 with prologue by Velimir Khlebnikov, libretto by Aleksei Kruchenykh (Olga Rozanova's partner), music by Mikhail Matiushin, design and costumes by Kasimir Malevich and lithographed poster by Olga Rozanova. It was remounted in 1983 in Los Angeles and a video of that production was shown at the Estorick Gallery in London in 2007. See John Milner, *A Slap in the Face! Futurists in Russia*, London 2007.

Parachute Lines - *USSR in Construction* was a lavish monthly government propaganda magazine in French, English, German and Russian (and a few in Spanish) between 1930 and 1941 to promote a favourable image of the USSR and its achievements. Victor Margolin calls it 'one of the most visually exciting magazines of the 20th century, thanks to an expansive budget … inventive layouts and photomontages, and the use of die-cuts, gatefolds and other experimental techniques.' Issue 12, 1935, the 'Parachute Issue', featured graphic design and photographs by Rodchenko and Stepanova. Komsomol - Communist Union of Youth

A Dream of 33 Letters – The Russian Cyrillic alphabet has 33 letters. Writers and artists met at the Stray Dog Café in St Petersburg, 1911-1915. Velimir Khlebnikov, Russian poet (b. 1885, d. 1922), called himself 'King of Time' and 'President of Planet Earth'.

Compasses: A Triptych - Based on photographs of Stepanova by Rodchenko, her 1920 self-portrait and other paintings, and excerpts from her journal – all in Bowlt and Drutt, eds., *Amazons of the Avant-Garde*, 1999. The John Donne quotation is from 'A Valediction: Forbidding Mourning'.

Popova's Turn - Liubov Popova (1889-1924) painted dozens of *Spatial Force Constructions* on plywood. She taught at Vkhutemas with Stepanova, Rodchenko and others. Both Popova and her five-year-old son died of scarlet fever in May 1924. Lenin died in January 1924.

Parsing the Ancestors - Epigraph is from Tsvetaeva's 'The Poet, Part 1' (1923) trans. Elaine Feinstein. Some of the imagery in my poem is also inspired by Part 1 of Tsvetaeva's poem. My notion of humans as half-flesh, half-wonder, is from the Finnish for human being, *ihminen*, 'one who wonders'.

Kaministiquia – Ontario village near Thunder Bay settled by numerous Finns.

Blaise Cendrars' poem 'La Prose du Transsibérien' presents a train journey across Russia which is dislocated in time and space by the narrator's free-flowing images, stories and memories. His companion, little Jehanne of Paris, keeps asking 'are we really far from Montmartre?'

Moosomin – Saskatchewan village near the farming settlement of New Finland, where my grandparents homesteaded.

Head-Smashed-In-Buffalo-Jump – a site in southwestern Alberta where the Cree ingeniously slaughtered herds of buffalo by driving them over cliffs. Now a UNESCO World Heritage Site.

Durak is a Russian card game, *scopa* an Italian one.

Tampere – Finnish city where Lenin and Stalin first met in 1905 in the workers' hall which now houses the Lenin Museum.

Amazon, Muse of Loss - The River Esk runs below Hawthornden Castle, a writers' retreat in Scotland where I had a month-long writing fellowship in 2007.

Fields of Vision – Epigraph is from a letter by William Blake to Thomas Butt, 22 November 1802.

Picklock – The Abloy company in Finland was founded in 1907 by Emil Henriksson, who designed its famous disc-detainer lock.

Viipuri (Vyborg in Russian) the largest city on the Karelian isthmus, was ceded by Finland to Russia after the Winter War of 1940-41 and the Continuation War of 1941-44.

No Broken Eggs, No Omelette – The brutal cliché in the title has been attributed to Lenin, Stalin, and Comrade Kaganovich, who said 'Why wail over broken eggs when we are trying to make an omelette!' (1932).

Hobo's Blood - The word 'utopia' is derived from the word 'nowhere'. Lisi uses the term 'hoopon veri' (hobo's blood) in her letter of 15 August 1936.

Letter from Somewhere, 1932 – The traditional 'beautiful corner' or 'red corner' in Russian houses held icons, candles, crosses and other Orthodox religious items. In Soviet times the red corner was used for images of political leaders, propaganda, etc.

Sister to Sister, 1935 - Some lines in this poem are verbatim from a letter by Lisi – the couplets and part of stanza five.

Song of the Shock Worker - Shock workers ('udarniki' in Russian, 'iskuri' in Finnish) were given prizes for working far beyond their quota.

'Life has improved, comrades. Life has become more joyous. And when life is joyous, work goes well.' … 'Are we really going to worship our backwardness and turn it into an icon, a fetish? … Have we ever taken an oath of loyalty to our backwardness?' – Stalin, address to the conference of Stakhanovites (shock workers), 17 November 1935. In that year Aleksei Stakhanov broke all records for the number of tons of coal mined by one person in a single shift.

Pencil and Blot - The famous Soviet clown Mikhail Rumyantsev first took the stage name Karandash in 1935 at the Leningrad State Circus, which Lisi and 40 other women shock workers attended that year.

Writing Spree, 1935 - Four lines in this poem are verbatim from a letter by Lisi.

Pencil Stubs - The White Sea Canal ('Belomorkanal' in Russian), 227 km through Karelia from the White Sea to Lake Onega, was constructed between 1931 and 1933 by over 100,000 Gulag prisoners; an estimated 10,000 or more died in the process. *USSR in Construction* No. 12, 1933, the 'White Sea Canal Issue', featured photographs by Rodchenko, as did the 1934 book edited by Maksim Gorky which eulogized the project. Posters and photographs of the project are in David King's book *Red Star over Russia: A Visual History of the Soviet Union from 1917 to the Death of Stalin*, London, Tate, 2009. Belomorkanal cigarettes could be bought in Russia in 2010 at 12 roubles for a pack of 20 (about 30 p).

Godmother - It is remotely possible but highly unlikely that my great-aunt Lisi had a child. This poem was written before her letters were uncovered in 2009.

Peter's Factory Town, 2010 – The literal meaning of Petrozavodsk is 'Peter's Factory'. Both Petrozavodsk and St Petersburg were founded by Peter the Great in 1703.

Legacy – Epigraph from Eeva-Liisa Manner, 'Assimilation' (1966) trans. Ritva Poom.

At Kondopoga, Lake Onega – The pulp and paper mill at Kondopoga (Kontupohja in Finnish) was the largest in the Soviet Union. It still operates.

In Job 40:15 the behemoth is a huge creature that eats grass like an ox.

The Orthodox priest of the Church of the Dormition in Kondopoga was executed in 1937. The literal meaning of Theotokos is 'God-bearer' or 'Birth-giver to God'. As is traditional, the icon of the Dormition of the Theotokos shows her on her deathbed surrounded by apostles and angels, with Christ holding a small child clothed in white representing the soul of the Virgin Mary.

Seen Not Heard - Reijo Kela's *Hiljainen Kansa (Silent People)* can be found in a field outside Suomussalmi, Finland, near the Russian border.

To Quest is Human - The first line is from Jeanette Lynes' poem 'The Road to Rosslyn Chapel,' in *The New Blue Distance*, Wolsak and Wynn, Hamilton, Ontario, 2009.

Simultaneity II - The Scottish castle library is at Hawthornden International Writers' Retreat.

Disappearance - The 'hay moon' is *heinäkuu*, July, when Lisi wrote her last surviving letter in 1939.

Night Train to St Petersburg - Epigraph from Akhmatova's 'The Moon in the Zenith – Drafts of a Long Poem on Central Asia, Part 9' (1942-44) trans. Richard McKane.

'Seven times seventy' – Matthew 18:21-22

Double - The girl on page 219 of the *Moscow Tourist Guide* 1967 is gazing at Karl Briullov's 1832 painting 'The Horsewoman'. It is remotely possible but highly unlikely that my great-aunt Lisi had a granddaughter.

My inner pedant would like to list everything I read as background for this book, but I turned most often to *Amazons of the Avant-Garde* edited by Bowlt & Drutt, *Origins of the Russian Avant-Garde* edited by Petrova & Horowitz, *Red Star over Russia: A Visual History of the Soviet Union from 1917 to the Death of Stalin* by David King, *The Russian Experiment in Art* by Camilla Gray and *A Slap in the Face! Futurists in Russia* by John Milner – all fully cited in my notes – as well as the following:

Akhmatova, Anna, *Selected Poems* (tr. Richard McKane, Bloodaxe, 1989);

Baron, Stanley & Jacques Damase, *Sonia Delaunay: The Life of an Artist* (Thames & Hudson, 1995);

Bowlt, John & Olga Matich, eds., *Laboratory of Dreams: The Russian Avant-Garde and Cultural Experiment* (Stanford U Press, 1996);

Cendrars, Blaise, *Complete Poems* (tr. Ron Padgett, U California Press, 1992);

Ciepiela, Catherine & Honor Moore, eds., *The Stray Dog Cabaret: A Book of Russian Poems* (tr. Paul Schmidt, NY Review Books, 2007);

Compton, Susan P., *The World Backwards: Russian Futurist Books 1912-16* (British Library, 1978);

Etkind, Alexander, 'Post-Soviet Hauntology: Cultural Memory of Soviet Terror' in *Constellations: An International Journal of Critical and Democratic Theory*, 16(1), 2009, 182-200;

Figes, Orlando, *Natasha's Dance: A Cultural History of Russia* (Penguin, 2002);

Harpelle, Ronald, Varpu Lindström & Alexis Pogorelskin, eds., *Karelian Exodus: Finnish Communities in North America and Soviet Karelia during the Depression Era* (Aspasia, 2004);

Janacek, Gerald, *Zaum: The Transrational Poetry of Russian Futurism* (San Diego State U Press, 1996);

Khlebnikov, Velimir, *Selected Poems* (tr. Paul Schmidt, ed. Vroon, Harvard U Press, 1997);

Lavrientev, Alexander, *Varvara Stepanova: A Constructivist Life* (Thames & Hudson, 1988);

Lodder, Christina, *Russian Constructivism* (Yale U Press, 1983);

Milner, John, *Dictionary of Russian and Soviet Artists* (Antique Collectors' Club, 1993);

Perloff, Marjorie, *The Futurist Moment* (U Chicago Press, 2003);

Rodchenko, Aleksandr, *Experiments for the Future: Diaries, Letters, Essays and Other Writings* (NY Museum of Modern Art, 2005);

Savander, Mayme, with L. Hertzel, *They Took My Father! A Story of Idealism and Betrayal* (Pfeifer-Hamilton, 1992);

Saxberg, Kelly, dir., *Letters from Karelia* (National Film Board of Canada, 2004, DVD from Aspasia Books & online at http://www.nfb.ca/film/letters_from_karelia).

Sebag Montefiore, Simon, *Stalin: The Court of the Red Tsar* (Weidenfeld & Nicolson, 2003);

Tsvetaeva, Marina, *Selected Poems* (tr. Elaine Feinstein, Carcanet, 1999);

Yablonskaya, M. N., *Women Artists of Russia's New Age 1900-1935* (tr. & ed. Anthony Parton, Thames & Hudson, 1990).

To Paul & Gail,

MORE GLIMPSES

with best wishes,

Hugh.